DANIEL CHALLIS

Guided Meditation for Wealth Attraction

A Journey to Cultivate Wealth, Increase Motivation, and Manifest Abundance

First edition

This book was professionally typeset on Reedsy.
Find out more at reedsy.com

It is the heart that makes a man rich. He is rich according to what he is, not according to what he has.

— HENRY WARD BEECHER

Contents

1

Manifesting Abundance

Welcome, dear listener, to "Guided Meditation for Wealth." As you settle into this moment, we invite you to embark on a transformative journey that will lead you to the very depths of your mind, unlocking the infinite potential within you to attract prosperity and wealth.

In this guided meditation, we will directly explore the vast and untapped power of your mind. Together, we will align your thoughts, emotions, and intentions, allowing you to manifest abundance in all facets of your life. This isn't just about material wealth; it's about fostering an abundance mindset that enriches every aspect of your existence.

This journey is an invitation to recognize and nurture your inner resources, ultimately leading to a life that is abundant in joy, satisfaction, and purpose. Through this meditative voyage, we will tap into a realm of limitless possibilities, where your desires resonate harmoniously with the universe.

So, let us begin this journey together. With an open heart and a receptive mind, let's set sail towards cultivating a mindset of abundance and unlocking the prosperity that is waiting for you. Welcome to this transformative experience. Let's begin.

2

Setting the Stage

Before we delve into our meditative journey, it is essential to set the stage for a serene and enriching experience. Creating the right environment is a crucial step in ensuring that your meditation is effective and transformative.

Begin by finding a quiet and comfortable space where you can sit or lie down without any disturbances. This space should be your sanctuary, a place where you can retreat from the demands of the outside world and focus inward. Ensure that you won't be interrupted, allowing yourself the freedom to fully immerse in this experience.

Once you've found your space, take a moment to adjust the lighting. Dimming the lights can help create a calming atmosphere, signaling to your mind that it's time to relax and unwind. If you'd like, you may also light a candle. The gentle flicker of the flame can serve as a soothing focal point, guiding you deeper into a state of relaxation.

Consider playing some soft, ambient music in the background. Gentle, calming sounds can enhance your meditation experience, creating an auditory landscape that facilitates introspection and mental clarity.

Take a few moments to settle into your space. Adjust your seating or lying position to ensure you are comfortable and at ease. Take a deep breath, allowing the calming ambiance to envelop you.

With your environment now set, you are ready to embark on this journey of manifesting abundance. Let us create an inner sanctuary conducive to introspection, relaxation, and transformation.

As we conclude Chapter 1, take a moment to reflect on the steps you've taken to set the stage for your meditation. To deepen your understanding and commitment to this practice, consider the following questions:

Describe the space you have chosen for your meditations. What makes this space special and conducive to relaxation and introspection for you?

How did you adjust the lighting, and what impact did this have on your mood and readiness to meditate? If you used a candle, how did its presence and flicker affect your sense of calm?

Reflect on the choice of ambient music or sounds you selected. How did these sounds contribute to creating an immersive meditative environment?

In what ways did you ensure your physical comfort during meditation? How did adjusting your position or surroundings help in enhancing your focus and relaxation?

As you settled into your meditation space, what thoughts and feelings arose? How did you manage these initial reactions to create a mindset conducive to meditation?

What are your expectations from this meditative journey? What intentions have you set for your practice of manifesting abundance?

Engaging with these questions will help you create a mindful approach to your meditation practice, ensuring each session is as effective and transformative as possible. Remember, the quality of your meditation is greatly influenced by the care and attention you give to preparing your environment and mindset.

3

The Breath of Wealth

As we move forward in our journey, let's turn our attention to the foundation of our meditation: the breath. The breath is a powerful tool, serving as a bridge between the mind and body, and it can be harnessed to attract wealth and abundance into our lives.

Close your eyes gently and turn your focus inward. Allow the external world to fade away as you bring your attention to your breathing. Start by taking deep, slow, and deliberate breaths. Feel the air entering your body, filling your lungs, and then slowly leaving you as you exhale.

As you breathe in, imagine that you are inhaling prosperity in the form of a radiant golden light. This light represents wealth, success, and abundance. Visualize this golden energy filling every cell of your body, infusing you with a sense of possibility and positivity.

With each exhale, release any doubts, fears, or limiting beliefs that may be holding you back. Let go of any thoughts of scarcity or lack. Envision these negative energies being expelled from your body, making space for the abundant energy you are inviting in.

Continue this cycle of breathing – inhaling prosperity and exhaling doubts. Feel the rhythm of your breath and the flow of golden energy coursing through you. With each breath, you are aligning yourself more closely with the energy of abundance.

Allow yourself to be immersed in this process, feeling a sense of wealth and prosperity growing within you. The Breath of Wealth is a practice of cultivating abundance from within, setting the stage for manifesting it in the external world. Let's continue to breathe and embrace the wealth that flows to us and through us.

After engaging in the Breath of Wealth meditation, take some time to reflect on your experience and deepen your connection with the practice.

How effective was the visualization of inhaling prosperity as a radiant golden light for you? Did this imagery enhance your sense of connection to wealth and abundance?

What doubts, fears, or limiting beliefs did you find yourself releasing with each exhale? How did it feel to let go of these negative energies?

Did you notice any physical sensations in your body as you practiced the Breath of Wealth? How did your body respond to the inhalation of prosperity and the exhalation of doubts?

What emotions arose during this meditation? Did you feel a shift in your emotional state from the beginning to the end of the practice?

How did the practice of breathing in wealth and exhaling doubt affect your sense of alignment with abundance? Did you feel more connected to the energy of wealth by the end of the meditation?

How has this meditation influenced your mindset towards manifesting wealth? Do you feel more prepared and open to receive abundance in your life?

What insights or realizations emerged during this meditation? Were there any moments of clarity or profound thought that you would like to explore further?

Taking the time to answer these questions can enrich your meditation experience, allowing you to fully absorb the lessons and energies of the Breath of Wealth practice. Remember, the journey to attracting wealth is as much about internal alignment as it is about external actions.

4

The Garden of Prosperity

Now that we have attuned ourselves with the Breath of Wealth, let us journey to a place within our minds that is fertile and ripe for manifesting abundance. Picture in your mind's eye a lush, thriving garden, teeming with life and vibrancy. This garden represents your mind – a space ready and waiting for the seeds of wealth and prosperity to be planted and nurtured.

As you imagine yourself walking through this garden, take note of the variety of plants and flowers surrounding you. Each plant, each bloom, symbolizes different aspects of your life – your relationships, career, health, passions, and dreams. Observe how each plant is unique, yet contributes to the overall beauty and harmony of the garden.

The soil beneath your feet is rich and nurturing, signifying the fertile ground of your mind, ready to cultivate the seeds of abundance. Feel the softness of the earth, the freshness of the air, and the warmth of the sunlight gently caressing your skin.

In this Garden of Prosperity, you have the power to cultivate and grow the wealth you seek. As you stroll through the garden, visualize yourself planting seeds along the path. These seeds represent your goals, aspirations, and desires for financial prosperity and abundance in all areas of your life.

See yourself nurturing these seeds with positive thoughts, affirmations, and actions. Watch as they take root, sprout, and grow into strong, healthy plants, bearing fruits and blossoms of success and fulfillment.

Allow yourself to feel a sense of joy and accomplishment as you witness your garden flourishing. Understand that just like this garden, your mind is a space of limitless potential, where you can cultivate and manifest all the prosperity you desire.

Take a moment to bask in the beauty and abundance of your Garden of Prosperity, knowing that you have the power to nurture and grow your wealth from within. Let's continue to cultivate this abundant mindset as we progress in our journey.

As you reflect on your journey through the Garden of Prosperity, consider these interactive questions to connect with the meditation:

How vividly were you able to visualize the Garden of Prosperity? Which aspects of the garden resonated most strongly with you?

Each plant and flower in the garden represents different aspects of your life. Which plants did you visualize as representing your career, relationships, health, and other key areas? How did you feel about these representations?

What emotions surfaced as you walked through your garden? Did you experience feelings of hope, joy, tranquility, or something else?

When you visualized planting seeds in your garden, what specific goals, aspirations, or desires did these represent? How did it feel to nurture these seeds in your mind's garden?

As you saw the seeds sprouting and growing, how did your perception of your ability to manifest wealth and success change?

What personal insights or revelations did you experience while in your Garden of Prosperity? Did the meditation bring clarity to any aspect of your life or goals?

How can you continue to nurture and care for your garden outside of meditation? What actions or thoughts can you incorporate into your daily life to support the growth of your goals and dreams?

Reflecting on these questions can help solidify the experience of the Garden of Prosperity meditation, allowing you to carry its lessons and energies into your daily life. Remember, the garden is a symbol of your own mind's potential to cultivate and manifest abundance in all forms.

5

Planting Seeds of Abundance

As you continue your journey through the Garden of Prosperity, you find in your hand a collection of seeds. These are not ordinary seeds, but seeds of prosperity, each one holding the potential to grow into a reality filled with abundance and wealth.

Take a moment to observe these seeds in your hand. Feel their texture, their weight, and recognize the boundless potential that lies within each one. These seeds represent your goals, aspirations, and desires related to wealth and prosperity.

Now, bend down and gently plant these seeds into the rich, nurturing soil of your garden. As you do so, visualize each seed as a specific financial goal or desire. Perhaps one seed represents the aspiration for a new job or a promotion. Another seed could symbolize a successful business venture, while yet another embodies your quest for financial freedom and security.

As you plant each seed, take a moment to clearly visualize your goal. Picture yourself in that new job, feel the joy of running your successful business, or experience the peace that comes with financial freedom. Allow these images to be vivid and filled with emotion, as this will nurture the seeds you are planting.

Envision the roots of these seeds growing deep into the soil, anchoring themselves firmly. Imagine the shoots sprouting upwards, reaching for the sunlight, and blossoming into fruition. With each day, these plants grow stronger, healthier, and more vibrant, much like your goals steadily transforming into reality.

Understand that these seeds of abundance, once planted, require nurturing and care. They need your attention, belief, and positive action to flourish. Trust that as you tend to your garden, providing it with love, dedication, and perseverance, your seeds of abundance will grow and bring forth the prosperity you seek.

In this chapter of our journey, embrace the power you have to manifest your desires. By planting your Seeds of Abundance, you are actively participating in the creation of your prosperous future. Let's continue to nurture these seeds and watch as our garden of prosperity flourishes.

As you engage with the practice of planting your Seeds of Abundance, these interactive questions can help you delve deeper into your meditation experience and apply its principles to your life:

What specific goals or aspirations did you choose to represent with your seeds of prosperity? Why were these particular goals important to you?

How vividly were you able to visualize planting your seeds and seeing them grow? Describe the images, feelings, or sensations that accompanied this process.

What emotions arose as you planted each seed? Did you feel hope, anticipation, excitement, or perhaps some fears or doubts?

How did each seed's growth in your visualization correlate with your real-life aspirations? Did some seeds grow faster or appear more vibrant than others?

What actions or steps can you take in your daily life to 'nurture' these seeds? How can you ensure that your goals and aspirations receive the attention and effort they need to flourish?

Did you encounter any challenges or obstacles in your visualization? How did you address them, and what does this reflect about your approach to obstacles in real life?

How did you feel visualizing your goals coming to fruition? How does this exercise influence your feelings and beliefs about your ability to achieve financial success and abundance?

How can you apply the principles of planting and nurturing seeds of abundance in your everyday life? What mindset shifts or practical steps can you take to align more closely with your vision of prosperity?

Reflecting on these questions can deepen your understanding and con-nection to the process of manifesting wealth and prosperity. Remember, the act of planting seeds in your meditation is a powerful metaphor for setting intentions and taking steps toward achieving your financial and personal goals.

6

Nurturing Your Wealth

Having planted your Seeds of Abundance in the fertile soil of your mind's garden, it is now time to nurture and care for them. Just as a garden needs water, sunlight, and care to thrive, so do your seeds of prosperity need attention, effort, and nurturing.

Visualize a gentle, nurturing rain beginning to shower your garden. The droplets of water softly caress the soil, seeping into the ground to reach the seeds you've planted. This rain symbolizes the actions, efforts, and positive energy that you invest in achieving your financial goals.

The rain could represent various things – it could be the time you spend enhancing your skills, the effort you put into networking, the diligence in managing your finances, or the courage to take calculated risks in your professional endeavors. Each drop is a step you take towards manifesting your wealth and abundance.

As the nurturing rain continues to fall, watch as your garden begins to transform. The seeds you've planted start to sprout, breaking through the soil and reaching toward the sky. Tender leaves unfurl, and soon, the plants grow stronger and taller, each one a representation of your goals and desires taking shape.

You see your garden blossoming with abundance – the plants bear fruits, the flowers bloom, and the air is filled with a sense of accomplishment and prosperity. Your efforts, symbolized by the nurturing rain, have allowed your seeds of wealth to grow and thrive.

Take a moment to walk through your transformed garden, witnessing the fruits of your labor. Understand that the journey to wealth and abundance is an ongoing process of planting, nurturing, and harvesting. Feel a sense of pride and joy in knowing that your efforts are coming to fruition.

In this chapter, embrace the understanding that nurturing your wealth is a continuous journey. By consistently putting in effort and cultivating a positive mindset, you are ensuring that your Garden of Prosperity remains lush and abundant. Let's continue to nurture our wealth as we progress in our meditative journey.

To deepen your engagement with the concepts presented in this chapter, consider reflecting on the following interactive questions:

Identifying Nurturing Actions: What specific actions or efforts does the nurturing rain in your visualization represent in your life? How are these actions contributing to your financial goals?

Personal Growth: As you visualized the rain nurturing your garden, what personal qualities or skills do you think you need to develop or enhance to achieve your financial aspirations?

Emotional Connection: How did you feel witnessing the growth and transformation of your garden under the nurturing rain? What emotions does this evoke about your journey towards financial prosperity?

Challenges in Nurturing: What challenges or obstacles might you face in consistently nurturing your Seeds of Abundance? How do you plan to overcome these challenges?

Visualization and Reality: How closely does your visualization align with your current efforts toward financial success? Are there any discrepancies, and if so, what might they indicate?

Action Steps: Based on your visualization, what immediate steps can you take in your daily life to nurture your financial goals? How can you integrate these actions into your routine?

Reflection of Efforts: In what ways do you see your current efforts and actions reflected in the growth and health of the plants in your garden? Are there any areas that need more attention or a different approach?

How do you envision the long-term nurturing of your financial goals? What practices or habits will you need to maintain to ensure continued growth and abundance?

By pondering these questions, you can gain deeper insights into your meditative journey and how it correlates with your real-world actions and aspirations. Remember, the process of nurturing your wealth is ongoing and requires consistent attention and effort. Use these reflections to guide and motivate your journey toward financial prosperity.

7

Harvesting Success

In this chapter of our guided meditation, we find ourselves standing in our flourishing Garden of Prosperity. The seeds you've planted and nurtured have grown into vibrant plants, each laden with fruits ripe for the picking. It is now time to reap the rewards of your efforts and to joyfully harvest the fruits of your garden.

Visualize yourself moving through your garden, your hands reaching out to gently pluck the fruits from the branches and vines. Each fruit that you gather is a successful manifestation of your financial goals and dreams. Perhaps one fruit represents the achievement of landing your dream job, another symbolizes the thriving state of your business, and yet another embodies your attainment of financial stability and freedom.

As you collect these fruits of success, feel the joy and satisfaction swelling in your heart. Your diligent efforts, positive mindset, and unwavering belief have brought you to this moment of harvest. Each fruit is a testament to your journey, and as you hold them, you can feel their weight, texture, and vibrancy.

Take a moment to express gratitude. Feel thankful for the abundance that you have manifested and for the journey that has led you here. Allow this feeling of gratitude to fill your heart, knowing that this positive energy will continue to nourish your garden and your life.

As you walk through your garden, basket laden with the fruits of your labor, you realize that this process of planting, nurturing, and harvesting is cyclical. With every goal achieved, a new seed of aspiration can be planted, and the cycle of abundance continues.

In this chapter of Harvesting Success, understand that your journey toward wealth and prosperity is both a destination and a continuous journey. Feel empowered knowing that you have the tools and the mindset to manifest abundance in all areas of your life. Let's carry this sense of accomplishment and readiness to continue our journey in the chapters to come.

At the end of this chapter, take a moment to reflect on your journey and the lessons learned with these interactive questions:

What specific achievements or successes do the fruits in your garden represent in your life? How do they correlate with your financial goals and dreams?

As you visualized harvesting the fruits, what emotions did you experience? How does this emotional response reflect your feelings about your real-life accomplishments?

Reflect on the things you felt grateful for during the meditation. How does practicing gratitude impact your perspective on wealth and success?

With every goal reached, what new aspirations or 'seeds' do you plan to plant in your garden of prosperity? How does this symbolize your ongoing journey towards financial abundance?

What important lessons have you learned during the process of planting, nurturing, and harvesting your goals? How will these lessons influence your future actions?

Reflect on the challenges you faced while nurturing your garden. How did overcoming these challenges contribute to the success you are now harvesting?

How can you share the fruits of your success with others? What does this act of sharing teach you about the nature of abundance and prosperity?

What steps will you take to prepare for the next cycle of planting, nurturing, and harvesting in your journey towards wealth and prosperity?

How do you plan to sustain and build upon the successes you've achieved? What practices or habits will help maintain your garden of prosperity?

Engaging with these questions will help you integrate the experiences of your guided meditation into actionable insights and reflections on your path to wealth and abundance. Remember, your journey is both a series of destinations and an ongoing process, with each success paving the way for new opportunities and growth.

8

Cultivating a Wealth Mindset

In the tranquility of your abundant garden, having experienced the joy of planting, nurturing, and harvesting your dreams, you now come to understand an essential truth: wealth is not just about monetary gains, but it is, more profoundly, a mindset and an attitude that permeates all aspects of your life.

As you stand amidst your prosperous garden, take a moment to reflect on the feelings of success and abundance that surround you. Recognize that a true Wealth Mindset goes beyond the accumulation of material wealth. It is a holistic approach that encompasses gratitude, generosity, and a sense of abundance in every aspect of your life.

Begin by cultivating gratitude. Feel a deep sense of thankfulness for the opportunities, experiences, and resources you have. This gratitude doesn't just encompass your financial achievements but extends to your relationships, your health, and even the small joys of everyday life.

Next, embrace a spirit of generosity. Visualize yourself sharing the fruits of your garden with others, whether it be your time, resources, or knowledge. Understand that true wealth is also measured by the positive impact you can make in the lives of others.

Finally, cultivate a sense of abundance. Shift your mindset from one of scarcity, where you might feel you never have enough, to one of abundance, where you believe there is plenty for everyone, including yourself. Visualize your garden as ever-expansive, with enough bounty to share and still continue to thrive.

By cultivating a Wealth Mindset, you create a fertile ground for continuous growth, prosperity, and fulfillment. It is this mindset that transforms every experience into an opportunity and every challenge into a stepping stone towards greater abundance.

In this chapter, recognize that your journey toward wealth is not just a pursuit of financial success but a holistic approach to living a life of abundance, gratitude, and generosity. Let's carry this enriched mindset forward as we continue our meditative journey towards manifesting abundance in all its forms.

At the end of this chapter, engage deeply with your journey towards a wealth mindset through these reflective questions:

How do you define wealth in your life beyond monetary terms? What aspects of your life contribute to your sense of wealth and abundance?

Identify three non-material aspects of your life that you are grateful for. How does acknowledging these areas enhance your sense of abundance?

What are some ways you can or have shared your wealth (knowledge, time, resources) with others? How does this generosity enrich your own sense of prosperity?

Reflect on any scarcity mindset you might have. What steps can you take to shift towards an abundance mindset? How does this shift change your perception of wealth and success?

In what ways can you integrate the Wealth Mindset into all areas of your life – personal, professional, social, and spiritual?

How does a Wealth Mindset transform your view of opportunities and challenges in life? Can you think of a recent challenge that, when viewed through this mindset, becomes an opportunity?

How do you envision your Wealth Mindset evolving over time? What practices or habits will you cultivate to continue this growth?

How can you inspire or teach others about cultivating a Wealth Mindset? What impact do you think this could have on their lives and your own?

How do you plan to balance the pursuit of material wealth with the cultivation of non-material riches in your life?

These questions are designed to deepen your understanding and application of a Wealth Mindset, encouraging a holistic approach to prosperity that encompasses more than just financial success. Reflecting on these questions will help you integrate the principles of gratitude, generosity, and abundance into your everyday life, paving the way for a more fulfilled and prosperous journey.

9

Conclusion

As we gently draw our guided meditation to a close, it is time to transition back to the world around us, carrying with us the profound insights and sense of abundance we have cultivated in our inner garden.

Gradually, begin to bring your awareness back to your surroundings. Slowly become aware of the surface beneath you, the air around you, and the gentle rhythm of your breath. With each inhale and exhale, feel yourself becoming more present, and more grounded.

Now, gently and at your own pace, open your eyes. Take a moment to notice how you feel. You may find yourself feeling refreshed, empowered, and filled with a renewed sense of purpose. The journey you embarked upon in your mind's garden has sown seeds of positivity and abundance that you can nurture and grow in your everyday life.

Remember, the garden of prosperity lies within you, always ready to be tended and cultivated. By nurturing this internal space with positivity, gratitude, and a wealth mindset, you invite abundance and success to manifest in various aspects of your life.

As you move forward, carry with you the lessons and experiences from this meditative journey. Know that you have the power to cultivate wealth, not just in the financial sense, but in the richness of spirit, relationships, and personal growth.

Thank you for embarking on this guided meditation journey towards manifesting abundance. May your Garden of Prosperity continue to flourish and bring you joy, success, and fulfillment in all that you pursue.